ABSURD ADVERTS

Published and distributed by
TOBAR LIMITED
St. Margaret, Harleston, Norfolk, IP20 0TB, UK
www.tobar.co.uk

This edition printed 2006

Printed in China

ISBN 13: 978
ISBN 10: 1

D0966466

ABSURD
A·D·V·E·R·T·S

Some companies will try almost anything to get you to buy their products, and as a result of this, advertising has become big, big business – billion dollar billboard campaigns and slick television commercials assault us from every angle!

However, there is another side to advertising that isn't quite so 'glamorous'. From the classifieds in small town newspapers to hilarious mistakes in translation, these are the ads that do more harm than good – some people believe that there's no such thing as bad publicity but even they'd be forced to reconsider once they've clapped their eyes on the absurd adverts featured here.

There are personals that are much too personal, and ads for restaurants that are guaranteed to leave one with a nasty taste in the mouth. But most of all, there are laughs a plenty to be found in the cock-ups, double entendres and puns that fill this book.

ANIMALS

Our furry and feathered friends may seem an unlikely source of absurd adverts but, judging from the ads in this chapter, a new pet is more likely to provide laughs than companionship! As you will discover, some people are trying to sell pets while others are looking for lost furry friends – but all have the same hilarious results.

FREE
TO GOOD HOME

Beautiful 6 mo old male kitten –
orange and caramel tabby, playful,
friendly, very affectionate.
Ideal for family w/kids.

OR

Handsome 32 yr old husband –
personable, funny, good job, but
doesn't like cats.
Says he goes or the cat goes.

Come see both and decide which
you'd like.

Call Jennifer on 265 5543

Newspaper ad

LOST

Small apricot poodle.
Reward. Neutered.
Like one of the family.

Newspaper ad

FOR SALE

Three canaries of undetermined sex

Newspaper ad

FOR SALE

Eight puppies from a German Shepherd
and an Alaskan Husky

Newspaper ad

FOUND

Dirty white dog... looks like a rat... been with us awhile now... there'd better be a reward...

Newspaper ad

FREE
PUPPIES

NEW BREED

½ Cocker Spaniel

½ Sneaky neighbour dog

Newspaper ad

GREAT
DAMES
FOR SALE

Newspaper ad

Dog for sale

**Eats anything
and is fond
of children**

Newspaper ad

FREE

to good country home
3/4 Rottweiler,
1/4 Shepherd,
3 years old,
female, spayed,
very intelligent.

**Loves to eat
live rabbits
and kittens.**

Newspaper ad

Spay or Neuter
your best friend!

Vet ad

WEEKEND GIVEAWAY

Guaranteed
free child with falcon,
from 1 May-20 June.

**Advert outside
travel agents**

Cows, Calves Never Bred

Also one gay bull for sale...

Advert outside farm

HORSE MANURE
50p PER PRE-PACKED BAG
20p DO-IT-YOURSELF

Newspaper ad

Chocolate Labrador puppies
itches only

Newspaper ad

All birds going cheap!

Pet shop ad

Keep happy friendship with your pets

Japanese pet shop ad

Two female Boston Terrier puppies
7 wks old, perfect markings, 555-1234.
Leave mess.

Newspaper ad

German shepherd 85 lbs
Neutered. Speaks German. Free.

Newspaper ad

FREE
Yorkshire Terrier!
Eight years old.
Hateful little dog.

Newspaper ad

Newspaper ad

DATING

The course of true love never runs smoothly, and nowhere is that sentiment more true than in the personal classifieds of a newspaper or an online dating service. Judging from the following loved-up ads, it's obvious that honesty is not always the best policy, and perhaps a little white lie here and there could help a lonely heart's chances immeasurably! Also, poetic language does not always come across well and learning to spell and use basic grammar would improve the chances of these ads actually hitting their target no end... instead of making that potential date run away, shrieking with laughter.

So, did these lovelorn losers find the 'happy ever after'? We'll never know – but have a read and honestly ask yourself... would you reply to them?

MR RIGHT

Why am I having so much trouble finding you? Sometimes I ask myself, "What's wrong? Am I too picky? Do I meet the wrong men, send the wrong signals and say the wrong things? Or say the right things to the wrong men while sending mixed signals? Am I too aloof, too forward, too loud, too quiet, too something? Maybe I tortured small animals in a previous life, and I'm paying for it in this one...?"

Online personal ad

"There is a little place in the jumbled sock drawer of my heart where you match up all the pairs, throw out the ones with holes in them, and buy me some of those neat dressy ones with the weird black and red geometrical designs on them."

Newspaper ad

SWM old, fat, balding with many disgusting habits seeks SWF with money. Send pictures of your house, car and RV. This could be your lucky day.

Online personal ad

23-year-old good-looking guy already in a relationship but wanting to see if there is someone out there better.

Newspaper personal ad

I'M LOOKING

for someone who is pumped when I'm pumped, psyched when I'm psyched, and stoked when I'm stoked. Unfortunately, my last boyfriend was always psyched when I was pumped, stoked when I was psyched, and pumped when I was stoked. Are you ready to give 150 percent to your next relationship? If so, **BRING IT ON!!!**

NEMESIS WANTED: I'm 5'10, into kayaking, books and conversation by day; justice, honour and vengeance by night. Seeking arch-enemy or possibly crimelord or deformed megalomaniac. Call 020 **** ****

Hideous-looking, obese, smelly, ill-tempered, lazy, cowardly, complete liar seeks total opposite.

LOOKING FOR a drama-free woman without baggage. Please, no confused 'little girls'! I would love to meet a woman that cares about her health and does something other than sit on the couch, eating bon-bons while watching Oprah talk about how much weight she has gained. I have not seriously dated a woman since I was shot in 1999.

GOOD-LOOKING

**Athletic Notting Hill-based movie star millionaire seeks gullible stunner.
Call 020 **** ****

PATRIARCH of up-and-coming religion seeks altar girl.

MINT CONDITION: Male, born 1932, high mileage, good condition, some hair, many new parts including hip, knee, cornea, valves. Isn't in running condition, but walks well.

"My tern off has to be vidio games. i like them but if you spend more than an hour or two with the playstation a day don't call me. I want a relation ship not a child."

CONGRATULATIONS! You are the thousandth reader to pass this ad by. Your prize is to pay for dinner and listen to me b*tch about my university colleagues until pub turfing-out time. And no, you don't get sex. Ever. Ever, ever, ever. Sensitive Female, 38.

I RARELY DATE
and I assume this is because all the good men are either dead, married or still in puberty.

I'M LOOKING FOR
a life companion who will share mutual and reciprocal loving, affection, and a need to be in touch with every experience in our past, current and future lives. I value rituals that honor and celebrate the mystery of life and the Mystery of the Catwoman.

I LIKE eating mayonnaise and peanut butter sandwiches in the rain, watching Barney Miller reruns and licking strangers on the subway; you eat beets raw, have climbed Kilimanjaro, and sweat freely and often. Must wear size five shoes.

I AM NOT A GREAT

and bare a very simple life. Always I like transparent. Randomly I waste my grater part of time for finding friends on net/in a daily life is not true, I like to share my soreness with them, those are founded by me continuing for a long time, will be my friend or love.

Newspaper personal ad

MY PERFECT FIRST DATE: long dinner in a nice quiet restaurant followed by something fun like a movie, play, etc. OR a trip to Europe.

Newspaper personal ad

BURIED under a mountain of credit-card bills and debt from spending like Paris Hilton on a bender, I live in the lousy part of Jersey City. I am a runner and an actress, but I am forced to do bad interactive murder mysteries that I refer to as "leading parts in off-Broadway plays." Even though I run marathons, I still can't lose those few pounds. But I can probably kick someone to death with my legs of steel.

Online personal ad

I'M BEAUTIFUL,

lithe, and charming. So why do I need to place an ad? I'm greedy. The only thing that makes me happy is cash in my account. I know there are men out there who want a pretty young thing on their arm and who are willing to spoil them to keep them there. I want to meet those men. I can be your devoted girl, I can make your coworkers green with envy, I can charm my way into your boss's inner circle. I can be as good for you as you are for me. So let's make a deal.

Online personal ad

I AM A SUCCESSFUL, accomplished woman. Up until now I have devoted most of my time to my career and my dog. But after taking time to paws and reflect, I feel it's now time to add another creature to my life.

Newspaper personal ad

MINIMALIST
seeks woman

WHEN I WAS 30
my dates had to be young, slim, tall, handsome, rich and intelligent. Now I'm 64, they only have to know how to read and use the telephone!

I DON'T HAVE
a specific idea about the man I want to meet. But at minimum, I expect you to be at least one foot taller than me, confident, assertive with everyone but me, make at least $75,000 a year more than me, dress well (or at least be open to my stylist Paolo's suggestions), play golf (if not, my pro can always teach you), and drive a car that people won't sneer at.

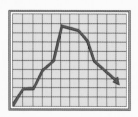

HELLO!

I am Neil, 52 years old and single. I have a 12-year-old daughter. However, my former wife disappeared with her two years ago somewhere in the Philippines. I am an insurance agent and have sold myself large amounts of life insurance, which is very important because I have prostate cancer that is expected to kill me within three years!

I AM **iro kalu ogbuagu** i was born in the eastern part of nigeria on the 19th of jun 1978. iam 5.10 meters tall. Iam a student, though i have not gotten money now i know i will have very soon. please show me picture of my white future wife. i want a woman who is earning about 25000 dollar or above i will like her also to help me to come over so that we can get married.

SBF Seeks Male Companionship

Age and ethnicity unimportant. I'm a young, svelte good looking girl who LOVES to play. I love long walks in the woods; riding in your pickup truck; hunting, camping, fishing trips. I love cozy winter nights spent lying by the fire. Candlelight dinners will have me eating out of your hand. Rub me the right way and watch me respond. I'll be at the front door when you get home from work, wearing only what nature gave me. Kiss me and I'm yours.

Call 555-XXXX and ask for Daisy.

The phone number was the Humane Society and Daisy was an eight-week old black Labrador Retriever. They received 643 calls in two days.)

MAN, honest. Will take anything.

Newspaper personal ad

FOOD & DRINK

We all love a good meal… unfortunately there are none to be found in this chapter devoted to the 'ad-solute' disasters of the food and drink business! Pretty much guaranteed to leave a bitter taste in your mouth, these mistakes in translation and perilous puns – not to mention the spelling and typographical errors – should come with a health warning!

With adverts taken from restaurants, cafés and shops plus newspapers, billboards and menus, there is a real selection for the discerning patron – but be warned, these ads may make you lose your appetite for good!

The noodles of a phantom with the resistance to the teeth of boast of our shop. The exquisite rainy season which repeated trial and error and was completed. Colourful red pepper of Asia. Domestic careful selection pork with little fat of female liking is used. It has healthy vegetables with salad feeling fully.

正沁圉

Ad for Japanese noodle bar

A superb and inexpensive restaurant

Fine foods expertly served by waitresses in appetizing forms

Restaurant ad

Hot beer
Lousy food
Bad service
Welcome

Pub sign

Dinner Special

Turkey	*$2.35*
Chicken or Beef	*$2.25*
Children	*$2.00*

Restaurant ad

SPECIALS EVERY DAY
(Monday-Wednesday)

Ad for Mexican restaurant

CREATIVE DAILY SPECIALS

including select offerings of beef, foul, fresh vegetables, salads and quiche.

Newspaper ad

No one really goes to Aqua Bar for the drinks, but we make sure our drinks won't kill you. This is something you must remember.

Ad for Japanese bar

Muesli bar offer
Buy one get one!

Health shop ad

7 ounces of choice sirloin steak, boiled to your likeness and smothered with golden fried onion rings.

Eat here and get gas

American service station sign

Newspaper ad

OUR WINES LEAVE YOU NOTHING TO HOPE FOR

Swiss restaurant wine list

All our eggs are made with three omelettes

New York café

20 dozen bottles of excellent Old Tawney Port, sold to pay for charges, the owner having been lost sight of, and bottled by us last year.

Newspaper ad

Win £5,000 cash!
No purchase necessary.
All details inside pack.

Turkey for sale
Partially eaten. Only eight days old.
Both drumsticks still intact. $23.00 ono.
Call 407 *** ***

Hang-O-Bar
Gonna be hangover
Free drink ¥5000

When you have felt thirst in your heart, you are in need of an oasis for quench your thirst. Your heart are thirsting for a good feeling of place.

Special today— no ice cream.

Don't stand there and be hungry, come in and get fed up.

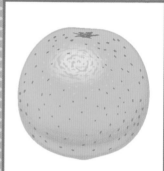

100% pure
all-natural,
fresh-squeezed
orange juice
from concentrate.

American café ad.

Newspaper ad

Tasty foods, fine drinks,
good music and nice
something at Booze-Up Bar!

Japanese bar billboard

The Lutheran men's group will meet at 6pm. Steak, mashed potatoes, green beans, bread and dessert will be served for a nominal feel. For those of you who have children and don't know it, we have a nursery downstairs.

Seven days without pizza makes one weak.

Now with two times more hydrogen than oxygen! Water that isn't watered down.

This is a multinational restaurant.
It can eat and drink till a morning.

Japanese restaurant ad

Burritos,
hat dogs
and the
best
tacos
in tawn!

Mexican restaurant ad

DONUT SHOP
Baked
'fresh' here!

American donut
shop billboard

'Pulkogi' which Mr Yamamoto produced is the most delicious food made use of special plate. 'Grilled udon' is good taste flavered with the juice of the Pulkogi-beef. It's satisfied with Korean Home Cooking Barbeque. Korean food is very healthy! Please roll it with Pulkogi in fresh Chisha and enjoy!! If you would eat your fill, you don't want long time. But that's Korean magic. You want to do it again!! Because you can't never forget magical Korean taste!!

Korean restaurant ad

OPEN 25 HOURS

Sign in bar in Germany

FOR SALE

Before internet auctions, people used to turn to local newspapers to sell their unwanted goods. However, as they couldn't afford access to a professional advertising team, their efforts were often sadly lacking in many, many areas as this chapter proves.

However, there is no such excuse for some of the businesses whose advertisements also appear in the following pages. Sometimes it may be the placers of the ads that are to blame. Some responsibility must also lie with the typesetters and proofreaders who let such howlers make their way into the pages of the local paper. But whoever is to blame is also the person to thank... for giving us all a good laugh!

If your car sounds like:

"Ping-click-ping"	$10.00
"Click-whine-click"	$25.00
"Clunk-whine-clunk"	$50.00
"Thud-clunk-thud"	$100.00
"Clang-thud-clang"	$300.00
"Can't describe it"	$500.00

Price list in Washington service station

DEAD COWS
on sale here!

Leather goods stall

BARGAIN BASEMENT
UPSTAIRS

London department store sign

For sale:
A quilted high chair
that can be made
into a table, pottie chair,
rocking horse,
refrigerator, spring coat,
size 8 and fur collar.

Newspaper ad

For Sale
Antique desk suitable
for lady with thick legs
and large drawers.

Newspaper ad

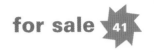
Modular Sofas

Only $299.00.
For rest or fore play.

Newspaper ad

WONDERFUL BARGAINS
FOR MEN WITH 16 AND 17 NECKS

Ad in clothing store

**For Sale
Bonsai tree
Large. £80.**

Call 020 **** ****

Newspaper ad

Full Size Mattress
Royal Tonic,
20 year warranty.
Like new.
Slight urine smell. $40.

Newspaper ad

Mixing bowl set
designed to
please a cook
with round bottom
for efficient beating.

Newspaper ad

Stuff
for sale here!

Garage sale sign

For sale:
King size rubber sheets,
black. £40/£45 clean.

Call 0161 *** ****

Newspaper ad

Wedding dress
used only once

Newspaper ad

Try our vacuums

They really suck!

Department store ad

We exchange anything!

Bicycles, washing machines, etc. Why not bring your wife along and get a wonderful bargain?

Ad in a secondhand shop

15 men's wool suits,

$10

They won't last an hour!

Ad in clothing store

Used tombstone, perfect for someone named Hendel Bergen Heinzel. One only.

FOR SALE: HOLIDAY PHOTOS Choice of ski, sun or city break. Ideal for anecdote or alibi. Call 020 **** ****

Order your

Summer Suit

Because of big rush we will execute customers in strict rotation.

Toaster

A gift that every member of the family appreciates. Automatically burns toast.

Ad in department store

Our bikinis are exciting

They are simply the tops.

Newspaper ad

Ladies and gentlemen
now you can have a bikini for a ridiculous figure.

Radio ad

For sale: One pair of hardly used dentures. Only two teeth missing. $100 obo.

Newspaper ad

See ladies blouses. 50% off!

LOGITECH WINGMAN JOYSTICK

$29.99

SAVE 1¢
List price $30.00

SAVE 1¢

Christmas tag-sale
Handmade gifts for the hard-to-find person.

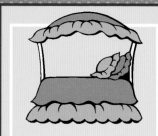

Four-poster bed, 101 years old.

Perfect for antique lover.

Sign in antiques shop

Sheer Stockings

Designed for fancy dress, but so serviceable that lots of women wear nothing else.

Newspaper ad

Ladies, don't forget the rummage sale. It's a chance to get rid of those things not worth keeping around the house. Don't forget your husbands.

Ad in church bulletin

Hitachi washing machine DX250, under warranty until kill kill kill,kill them all February 2004, in perfect working order. £180 ono. **Call 020 **** ****

Newspaper ad

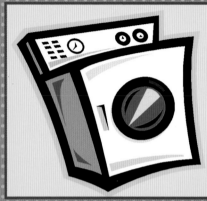

For Sale: Diamonds $20,00 Microscopes $15.00

Newspaper ad

FOR SALE BY OWNER

Complete set of Encyclopaedia Britannica. 45 volumes. Excellent condition. $1,000.00 or best offer. No longer needed. Got married last weekend. Wife knows everything.

New York Times classifieds

MONDAY (original ad)
For sale: R.D. Jones has one sewing machine for sale.
Phone 948-0707 after 7pm and ask for Mrs Kelly who
lives with him cheap.

TUESDAY
Notice: We regret having erred in R.D. Jones' ad
yesterday. It should have read, "One sewing machine
for sale cheap. Phone 948-0707 and ask for Mrs Kelly,
who lives with him after 7pm."

WEDNESDAY
Notice: R.D. Jones has informed us that he has
received several annoying telephone calls because of
the error we made in the classified ad yesterday. The ad
stands correct as follows: "For sale. R.D. Jones has
one sewing machine for sale. Cheap. Phone 948-0707
after 7pm and ask for Mrs Kelly who loves with him."

THURSDAY
Notice: I, R.D. Jones, have no sewing machine for sale.
I smashed it. Don't call 948-0707 as I have had the
phone disconnected. I have not been carrying on with
Mrs Kelly. Until yesterday she was my housekeeper but
she quit!

Ads and corrections that
appeared in a newspaper over
the course of four days

SERVICES

Rather than selling a product, some adverts exist to sell us a service, be it pest control, private tuition or plumbing. However, as this chapter amply demonstrates, some adverts don't exactly do their job well, and could actually drive a business into the ground instead of drumming up new customers! After all, when confronted by such idiocy, you'd never know what kind of service you might receive if you did decide to make that phone call...

Although some of the ads reproduced over the following pages are intentionally humorous and do a very good job of raising a giggle, more often than not it is the mistakenly funny ones that will really have you splitting your sides.

FED UP

of dieting and exercise?

Incredible results guaranteed!

- *Try amoebic dysentery!*
- *Vials available: £20.*
- *Simply add to seafood.*

CALL
020 **** ****

(shouldn't, but
may cause fatality)

Ad on lamp post in London

Am you Grammer [sic] letting we down? Private tuition available.

Now call now 07689 *** ***

Newspaper ad

Don't sleep with a drip. Call your plumber.

Ad on the trucks of a Pennsylvania plumbing company

No appointment necessary.
We'll hear you coming.

Ad outside American muffler shop

Tattoos done while you wait!

Money worries?
Work from home,
earn £££££££s!
You don't even have
to get out of bed!

**To find out more call
'Pimp' Jimmy on
020 **** ****

Our motto is to give our customers the lowest possible prices and workmanship.

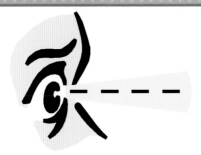

If you don't see what you're looking for, you've come to the right place.

Ad in an optometrist's window

Speech impediment? There's a new support group in the London area. Call D-DD-D-DDD-Dave on 020 **** ****

Newspaper ad

OPEN

seven days a week plus now open weekends!

Newspaper ad for a department store

FREE PICK-UP AND DELIVERY

Try us once, you'll never go anywhere again.

Ad for auto repair service

NOW IS THE PERFECT TIME TO GET YOUR EARS PIERCED AND GET AN EXTRA PAIR TO TAKE HOME, TOO!

Ad in beautician's window

Why go elsewhere and be cheated when you can come here?

In the window of an Oregon store

We take
your bags
and send them
in all directions

Copenhagen airline ad

Illiterate?
Write today
for free help

Newspaper ad

Don't kill your wife.
Let our washing machine do the dirty work.

In the window of a Kentucky appliance store

Get rich quick!
Simply set up a premium rate phone line. To find out how just call 0900 * *** ££££££**

Newspaper ad

Want a £50k income? Then ignore signs like this, go back to college, get some qualifications and become a solicitor.

College advertising poster in New York

Tired of cleaning yourself? Let me do it.

Newspaper ad

VACATION SPECIAL

Have your house exterminated.

Newspaper ad

We can repair your car after your cousin fixed it

Car repair shop ad

GET RID OF AUNTS:

ZAP DOES THE JOB IN 24 HOURS!

Newspaper ad

Best place in town to take a leak

Ad outside a radiator shop

Is your memory letting you down?

And what about your memory? Is it letting you down?

Call for information pack right now.

Before you forget.
079828 ******

Poster

Why go elsewhere to be cheated?
Come here first!

Poster in used car yard

We buy junk and sell antiques

Outside a county shop

We dispense with accuracy

New York pharmacy ad

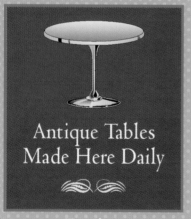

Antique Tables Made Here Daily

Furniture shop ad

We will sell gasoline to anyone in a glass container

Ad outside a Santa Fe petrol station

Ask about our plans for owning your home

In the offices of a loan company

Jimmy's Shoe Repair

- I will heel you
- I will save your sole
- I will even dye for you

Newspaper ad

Are you an adult who cannot read? If so, we can help.

Ad on a poster in Ghana

WANTED

We all want so much out of life. Some people need a professional to get them out of a tight spot, others just need the perfect practical product. Some place advertisements in newspapers or online to get that certain something and that's where the hilarity begins for the rest of us. Over the next few pages, you will see what happens when phrasing, double entendres and dodgy typing clash with the demands of some unfortunate individuals.

Again, it is unknown whether these adverts actually led to any of the advertisers fulfilling their wishes… but it's highly unlikely. After all, would you want to work for these people? Remember, all the following have been taken from real newspaper ads…

Newspaper ad

Wanted: Widower with school-age children requires person to assume general housekeeping duties. Must be capable of contributing to growth of family.

Newspaper ad

Wanted:
Mother's helper – peasant working conditions.

Newspaper ad

WANTED:
Used paint

Newspaper ad

Wanted
Unmarried girls to pick fresh fruit and produce at night

Newspaper ad

Wanted:
Part-time married girls for soda fountain in sandwich shop

Newspaper ad

Wanted:
Chambermaid in rectory. Love in, $200.00 a month.

References required.

Newspaper ad

Wanted

Man wanted to work in dynamite factory.

Must be willing to travel.

Newspaper ad

Wanted
Hair-cutter.
Excellent growth
potential.

Newspaper ad

Wanted: Man to take care of cow that does not smoke or drink.

Newspaper ad

Wanted

50 GIRLS FOR STRIPPING MACHINE OPERATORS IN FACTORY

Newspaper ad

Wanted:
Telescopic driver

- Must hold current certificate.
- Own transport.

Newspaper ad

Wanted
3-year-old teacher needed for pre-school.

Experience preferred.

WANTED
Preparer of food. Must be dependable like the food business, and be willing to get hands dirty.

WANTED
GIRL WANTED TO ASSIST MAGICIAN IN CUTTING-OFF-HEAD ILLUSION. BLUE CROSS AND SALARY.

Wanted

30 Chinamen and a zeppelin
for elaborate practical joke.

Can you help?
Please call on 07829 *** ***

Newspaper ad

Small minority wanted to spoil it for
the rest of us. There's always one –
is it you? Please call 020 *** ***

Newspaper ad

AND FINALLY

Some of the best things in life defy explanation. And that is also true in the wonderful world of amusing and absurd adverts. What follows is a mixed bag of mistakes and errors, bizarre spelling and punctuation 'experiments' as well as the occasional intentional joker.

Whether stupid or clever, witty or weird, do remember that all these ads are trying to appeal to you, the consumer. Although it may not be in the way the advertisers quite intended…

High school dropouts typically earn 42% less than high school graduates.

If you earn less than half the salary of a graduate, that means having 42% less of everything.

If you think you've seen everything in Paris,
visit the Pere Lachasis Cemetery.
It boasts such immortals as Moliere,
Jean de la Fountain and Chopin.

Tourism brochure

DO YOU LIKE BOWLING?

Let's play bowling.
Breaking down the pins
and get hot
communication.

Ad for bowling alley in Japan

This fathers' day have the kids shot!

Photo studio ad

For Rent
Six-room hated apartment

Newspaper ad

US computer company slogan

Be with us again
next Saturday at 10:00 pm
for High Fidelity,
designed to help music lovers
increase their reproduction.

Radio ad

Amanda

I'm running a bit late.
Will be there in about an hour.
How far apart are the contractions?

Newspaper ad

**Highly recommended
by owner!**

Sign outside motel

The hotel has bowling alleys,
tennis courts, comfortable beds
and other athletic facilities.

**This is the model home for your future.
It was panned by Better Homes & Gardens.**

Newbury Street Coiffure
AFFORDABLE
An Alternative to Looking Good

And now,
the Superstore –
unequaled in size,
unmatched in variety,
unrivaled
inconvenience.

Newspaper ad

Don't let worries kill you

Let the church help

Sign outside church

Mt. Kilimanjaro,

the breathtaking backdrop for the Serena Lodge.
Swim in the lovely pool while you drink it all in.

Tourism brochure

Roof leaks – Guaranteed

Ad for company that stops roof leaks

Junk yard poster

KIMCHI MUSEUM
OPEN HOUR

Japanese museum sign

Low self-esteem support group

meets this Tuesday.

Please use the side door.

Poster in church

Free Copy Machine — $0.25 Per Copy
Free Faxing — $1.25 Per Page

Ad in American hotel